CW00408998

INTERNATIONAL SCHOOL OF LONDON

130 Gunnersbury Ave.
London
W5 8LG

Tina Turner

by Kate Hammer

Picture Credits:
Bettmann: 6, 7 (right), 8, 12 (left), 15, 21, 23, 52, 53; **Capitol Records:** 18-19/Paul Cox, 27 (right)/Lorraine Day, 45/Paul Cox; **Gamma:** 31/Burrows, 46, 50-51 and 54, 55 (top); **Hulton Deutsch Collection Limited:** 13/Jacobson; **Images:** 14, 40 (left); **Katz Pictures Ltd:** 6-7 (middle) and 40 (right)/Brain Lanker; **The Kobal Collection:** 28 (left), 29, 38, 41; **London Features International Ltd:** cover, 9/Pantsios, 12 (right)/Paul Cox, 25 and 28/Michael Ochs, 32, 33, 35/Ebet Roberts, 37, 39/Michael Ochs, 48 Ken Regan; **Mirror Syndication International:** 4-5, 55 (bottom), 58-59; **Redferns:** 10/Max Jones, 11 (top)/David Redfern, (bottom)/William Gottlieb, 16 (left)/Robert Smith, (right)/Bob Willoughby, 24/Tom Hanley, 26 (left)/David Redfern, (right)/Tim Hall, 27 (left)/Fin Costello, 30, 34/David Redfern, 47 (left)/Richie Aaron; **Reuters/Bettmann:** 47 (right)/ Peter Morgan; **Roger Davies Management:** 49, 56-57; **Spectrum Colour Library:** 44; **Teamwork Productions Inc.:** 43/Dave Hogan.

The Publishers wish to thank Lucy O'Brien for the section on 'The changing role of women in pop' that appears on pp. 60-61.

Published in Great Britain in 1994
by Exley Publications Ltd,
16 Chalk Hill, Watford,
Herts WD1 4BN, United Kingdom.

Copyright © Exley Publications, 1994
Copyright © Kate Hammer, 1994

A copy of the CIP data is available from the British Library on request.

ISBN 1-85015-478-3

All rights reserved. No part of this publication
may be reproduced or transmitted in any form
or by any means, electronic or mechanical,
including photocopy, recording or any
information storage and retrieval system without
permission in writing from the Publisher.

Series editor: Samantha Armstrong
Editorial assistants: Helen Lanz and Alison
MacTier
Picture editors: Alex and Dora Goldberg of
Image Select
Typeset by Delta Print, Watford, Herts, U.K.
Printed in Hungary

Tina Turner

by Kate Hammer

 EXLEY

Queen of rock

One hundred and eighty-two thousand eyes are on the stage. Spotlights sweep the stadium. Tens of thousands of bodies inhale as she enters, gliding down a long staircase. The queen of rock is here. Her name is Tina Turner. She grabs the microphone, screams, and the fans go wild. Never have so many people come to see a single performer!

Tina Turner's journey to the Maracana Stadium in Rio de Janeiro in 1988, was longer than just a tiring plane flight. She had fought for more than record numbers of crowds and gold discs. Tina Turner had determinedly fought for her independence and self-esteem, escaped from her marriage to Ike Turner, and achieved success against all odds. Tina left her

Below: Anna Mae worked in the cotton fields when she was a girl. She dreaded cotton picking time and claimed that was part of her motivation for changing her life.

husband and risked losing her life's work in music, yet her solo career became more brilliant than any of her successes with Ike.

For a black woman to make it in a white man's world takes commitment, drive, talent, and courage. And Tina had all of these. When it came to achieving her dreams, Tina Turner's energy never failed. She has made numerous Top 100 hits, has had a score of

Previous page: Tina Turner takes the stage at the Maracana Stadium in Rio de Janeiro, Brazil, in 1988 – and she takes it alone. Twelve years after leaving Ike Turner, the queen of rock plays to a record crowd of 182,000 people – the largest audience ever assembled at this time for a single performer.

gold and platinum records with sales over 100,000 and 300,000 respectively, has starred in movies, has earned many Grammy awards for her music, and has won an acting award. This is the amazing story of Tina Turner's success.

Nut Bush city limits

Tina Turner began her life as Anna Mae Bullock on November 26, 1939. She was born in Brownsville, Tennessee in the United States. As Anna Mae, she spent her early childhood in the small town of Nut Bush. Forty-five miles (72 km) northeast of Memphis, along Highway 19, Nut Bush boasted a church, a school, a general store, and a night club.

Springing from the rich soil along the fertile valley of the Mississippi River, Nut Bush was most valued for its agriculture. As girls, Tina and her sister, Alline, would help their father pick and chop cotton and gather strawberries on the farm.

Tina's father, Floyd Richard Bullock, was an African American who was descended from slaves. He had a responsible position as manager of the

Left: Tina displays her gold and platinum records and her hit singles. These trophies were earned by four decades of tireless work in the entertainment industry. Tina's career grew beyond performing to include song-writing, choreography, producing, management and composing.

Below: Anna Mae grew up with a variety of musical influences around her. Gospel was one of those influences that enriched her musical background. The gospel sounds of the Metropolitan Community Church Choir of Chicago (pictured here) were popular enough to draw an audience of up to three thousand each Sunday.

sharecroppers who tended a large farm belonging to a white family. He also served as a deacon in the Woodlawn Baptist Church. Sharecropping had replaced slavery without disturbing the balance of power. White families owned the farmland, as they had done in the times of slavery, and hired black people at low wages to do the physical work.

Tina's mother, Zelma, also had Native American blood. Zelma's father was three-quarters Navajo and Zelma's mother was part Cherokee. Tina, then known as little Anna Mae, had the spirit and heritage of many peoples in her.

Looking back, Tina Turner said later, "I started out a girl in cotton fields, picking strawberries. A country girl. My family didn't own property, but we were always very clean, we had a roof over our heads and we always had seasonal clothes. And I had my dreams. My dreams came true."

Family breakup

When the United States entered World War II in 1941, Richard and Zelma Bullock joined thousands of people who lined up for the new jobs created by the war effort. They moved across the state to Knoxville to work on military bases.

For the two years that their parents worked in Knoxville, Alline and Anna Mae were separated. Anna Mae's first big blow was leaving Alline with their Native American grandparents, while she was sent off to live with her stern Baptist grandparents, the Bullocks.

One summer, the girls stayed with their parents in Knoxville for a few months. Anna Mae, at the age of four, delighted in the sights and sounds of the big city. While Zelma and Richard worked, Alline and Anna Mae were looked after by a fiercely religious woman, Mrs. Blake.

Mrs. Blake took the girls to church services. Unlike the stern worship in their father's church, here they joined in with the jubilant gospel singing and clapping. To the overflowing sounds of the piano, organ, and choir, some members of the congregation danced in the aisles. Sometimes, a

Moved by music, faith, and emotion, a woman cries out. As a child, Anna Mae witnessed such religious devotion. "I knew I could never be a part of that religion, really, but for a little girl, those sanctified services were something to see."

believer would slip into an ecstatic trance known as speaking in tongues. Alline remembered that, "one time Ann's underpants fell down around her ankles, she was dancing so hard. But she didn't let up." Back in Nut Bush, Anna Mae joined the choir at the Spring Hill Baptist Church.

The end of the war in 1945 brought the Bullock family back together again in Nut Bush. In the spring and summer months, the family would enjoy the picnics that drew the local community together to share homemade food and homegrown music. The group sang country songs, and Anna Mae, just seven or eight years old, was always ready to jump in. Some evenings, the Bullock family would drive out to the nearby town of Ripley, where the girls could see a

It was the vitality of Anna Mae, as well as the strength of her singing voice, that attracted Ike Turner. Ike may have renamed her Tina Turner, but it was Anna Mae who developed the power and personality of the Tina Turner image.

movie while their parents went to the clubs and bars. These were called "juke joints" because the music came from jukeboxes playing the latest singles.

The Savoy Ballroom in Harlem is all eyes, as a couple keeps the crowd entranced and clapping with their lively footwork. Social dance has always been democratic – it doesn't discriminate between rich and poor, city and country, black or white. All it takes is the sounds . . . and some free floor space!

Richard and Zelma fought bitterly and violently and, in 1950, when Anna Mae was eleven, Zelma left the family home and moved to St. Louis, leaving her children behind. "That's when it really hit me how much I loved my mother – and how much I hated her, too," Tina Turner was to remember later. "I guess I was learning how close love and hate can be. I wanted her to come back for Alline and me. And I waited, and waited, and she never did. I cried and cried, but it didn't do any good. It never does, you know."

A background of music

Anna Mae Bullock's childhood illustrates that one lifetime can contain many strands and influences. Her father's and mother's families, one strict Baptist, one Native American, were very different in Anna Mae's eyes. Mrs. Blake's church services in Knoxville were a far cry from the sober religion in her father's church. The picnic music of Nut Bush was not the gospel she sang in the Spring Hill choir, nor the steamy sounds of boogie-woogie that oozed from the juke joints. These differences made Anna Mae's life as rich as the soil she helped farm.

Anna Mae grew up in the jazz age, when African Americans were gaining international prominence for their excellence in improvised music. For as long as Africans have contributed to the mosaic of American culture, they have enriched its music.

In the 1700s and 1800s when Africans were captured and imprisoned as slaves to cross to the "New World" on boats, they were forced onto the ships' decks to sing and dance in their chains in order to stay fit. Untold numbers perished in these crossings, from starvation, physical abuse, and inhumane conditions. Those that survived brought the songs and dances of their African homelands with them to the shores of the United States.

In the United States, the slaves were introduced to Christianity and its musical traditions. Hymns were adapted for outdoor services, and songs were composed while the slaves worked the fields. They added rhythms, emphasis, and words or lyrics to reflect their point of view. Unlike the European musical tradition, which was written down and passed on to pupils through formal musical education, African American songs were passed down from person-to-person by word of mouth.

The music of one of the best-loved band-leaders in the United States, Count Basie, (above), and the great jazz singer Billie Holiday (below), influenced Anna Mae as she grew up.

Black music

Tina Turner's influences, then, were varied – from gospel to boogie-woogie to rhythm and blues. Boogie-woogie is played on both the piano and the guitar, although the term is also used to describe a way of playing the piano. The bass line, which is played by the left hand on the piano's lower keys, provides the melody, or tune.

Blues is a sister sound to boogie-woogie, but it is harder to define because there have been many blues sounds from different regions and decades. Blues evolved from the field songs the slaves sang. It uses the "call and response" structure used in church services. As blues changed, it was sold by record companies in what were called "race" magazines aimed at black buyers only. After World War II, this

type of music became known as "rhythm and blues," or R & B, and the guitars and pianos were electrified and amplified. The term R & B became a general term for music made by black artists and sold to black audiences.

Gospel, too, grew out of the religious traditions of African Americans, whose Christianity was influenced by older folk beliefs from Africa. It developed from hymns and spiritual songs and adopted the same subjects for its lyrics, but shook the sound up by adding a strong, off-beat syncopation. The stress would be placed on the weaker beat, as opposed to the stronger one. That syncopated rhythm was gospel's greatest contribution to the future of sound: the fusion of styles called rock and roll.

Above: In 1939, gospel star Marian Anderson was banned from singing in Constitution Hall in Washington, D.C., because she was black. A politician arranged for Ms. Anderson to sing on the steps of the Lincoln Memorial to protest the decision. Tens of thousands of people of all races and creeds attended the concert.

Free at last?

Racial segregation shaped Anna Mae's childhood, but she could see its limits and grew up to stretch beyond them. Slavery was abolished in the United States in 1865, but very little education, training, or resources were provided for the newly-freed African Americans.

In the southern states of America, segregation was imposed through laws that became known as "Jim Crow." Separate schools, restaurants, and prejudiced trading continually reinforced the unjust illusion of white superiority.

In 1954, a case came before the United States' Supreme Court that challenged segregation. But while the court ruled that segregation was illegal, it took decades longer to really undo all it had set in place. It may not have been legal from that date, but the realities of where people lived, the work they did, and where they went to school were still very much part of day-to-day life. It was difficult to fight because many people were unaware of their own prejudices about people whose skin, language, or religion was different from their own.

As Tina Turner, Anna Mae would overcome these barriers although she did not know her own potential at the time.

Growing pains

When Anna's mother, Zelma, moved to St. Louis it was the first of several big changes in eleven year old Anna Mae's life. Soon after, her father, Richard, remarried. That marriage quickly turned sour and the new wife left almost as quickly as she'd arrived. Alone again, Richard despaired.

When Anna Mae was thirteen, Richard picked himself up and moved to Detroit, leaving the girls in the care of his brother's mother-in-law, Ella Vera. Ella watched out for Anna Mae and Alline, but there was little love to soften the blows of rejection.

Worst of all for Anna Mae, her cousin and best friend, Margaret, was tragically killed in a car accident. "I can close my eyes," said Tina later, "and still see the pictures in the Ripley newspaper. They were so horrible. Margaret had been sitting in the front seat. When the car hit the truck, Margaret was thrown out and killed immediately."

City lights

In 1956, after two years at school in Brownsville, near Nut Bush, sixteen year old Anna Mae joined her mother in St. Louis. Alline was already living with Zelma. Anna Mae's grandmother had passed away,

Above: This sign was posted by African Americans to encourage black buyers to think about where they chose to live in order to promote integration. The southern states of America, where Anna Mae grew up, were slow to embrace the idea of integration and it was often difficult for black people to move into areas of their choice.

Opposite middle: Tina's roots in gospel and blues music prepared her well for the demands of the later sounds of rock. Here she shares the stage with blues guitarist, Robert Cray, known for his fine finger work and guitar riffs.

her high school sweetheart had married an old flame, and Nut Bush held little promise for a future beyond the cotton fields.

St. Louis was a metropolis compared with Brownsville and Ripley. The city stretched across the Mississippi River to the sister city of East St. Louis. East St. Louis was where things were happening. Anna Mae looked to her older sister, now nineteen, to show her the ropes.

Alline was working at a classy bar, where she earned a decent wage in tips. At night, she dressed up for her dates. One of her dates, Gene Washington, was the drummer for a band, the Kings of Rhythm. Together, Gene and Alline took Anna Mae for a night of music at a 250 seat club in East St. Louis, the Club Manhattan. It shook until dawn with the sounds of R & B. As the band warmed up, Tina recalled, "I was sitting there, a little bored, because this wasn't really my cup of tea, you know? Or at least I didn't think it was."

Then Ike Turner arrived – the man who was to shape Anna Mae's life into his own dream.

With time, Ike would become Anna Mae's guardian angel, musical mentor and manager,

Known as the "Gateway to the West," the city of St. Louis was founded as a French trading post in 1764. It was passed on to the United States in 1803. The Gateway Arch, built in 1965, overlooks the Mississippi River and is a memorial to the pioneers who settled the West. Anna Mae moved to the city in 1956 to join her mother, Zelma, and sister, Alline.

husband, and father to her sons. But life with Ike would not always prove to be easy. Anna Mae's future with Ike would test her talent, her patience, and her personal strength. In fact, she would prove that despite Ike, rather than because of him, Tina Turner could succeed – on her own – as the queen of rock!

Ike Turner

Ike Turner was the king of the Kings of Rhythm. He was the brains behind the whole operation: he played the guitar brilliantly and wrote the music for the band. "Ike was a genius," remembered saxophonist Eddie Shaw. At the Club Manhattan, the audience was filled with women; it was said that the men were there only to watch out for "their" ladies when Ike was playing.

Although Ike was by no means wealthy by the standards of the white-dominated entertainment world, he displayed all the trappings and elegance of success. His father was a preacher in the local church in Mississippi and, as a boy, he began plunking piano keys at a local churchwoman's house. After an excellent report card from his school, Ike's mother presented him with a piano of his own as a reward. But Ike was not one to play by the rules. Soon he was copying the songs he heard on the radio, teaching himself the rhythms and melodies of the latest bands and blues tunes. At sixteen, Ike was a disc jockey.

In 1951, Ike's band had recorded "Rocket 88" with a producer named Sam Phillips, who was later to become famous for launching the career of a young white singer, Elvis Presley. "Rocket 88" had stormed the charts and sold over a half a million copies, but the band members had earned little more than $20 each for their efforts! This was an early lesson for Ike in the injustices of the music business. In the school of setbacks, Ike was hit hard.

Instead of giving up, Ike went on to work harder, scouring the region for fresh talent, while staying busy priming his own band. He was aching to get ahead in the ruthless world of music.

A seasoned musician-manager, Ike Turner had toured the music circuits of the southern states of America with his band Kings of Rhythm. A determined man, Ike Turner was banking on making it big.

Above and right: Before families relied so much on television for information and entertainment, the radio played an important role in family life. It was the best way to popularize new songs and to introduce new bands to listeners. As records were promoted in this way, the record market exploded. It was through radio airplay that Ike Turner was eventually heard, with Anna Mae as lead vocalist. The success of their record "A Fool in Love" led to the creation of the Ike and Tina Turner Revue.

Behind the scenes

Most of the work to stardom goes on behind the scenes. Ike was quick to learn this. The music business had changed fast, as new technologies, new markets, new musical styles, and fresh new stars had been discovered. After the development of radio, the single greatest invention to affect music had been the record player. Before records were invented in the late nineteenth century, listeners were charged for sheet music, or written scores, and also at concerts. Every time a piece of sheet music was sold, some of the money went to the songwriter. Known as a royalty, this fee was how the songwriter made money. The sheet music industry continued in the United States until the 1950s.

By the end of World War II, records had become big business, selling more than $109 million worth in 1945, which was double the sales of 1941, despite wartime limits on materials. Radio had flourished, including black radio, with African American DJs defining each station's sound. Independent recording studios, or "indies," had also sprouted up to meet the huge demand for records. Most of these studios were owned by white people employing black artists.

Problems arose for songwriters like Ike Turner because sheet music virtually disappeared with the coming of radio. It became difficult to charge money to play records on the radio. So, to ensure the songwriter was paid, his or her fee had to be written into any record deals that were done with the record company.

Musical integration

By the 1950s, young people of all races were listening to similar sounds across the different music categories. Racially integrated teams of singers, musicians, songwriters, producers, and promoters worked together to make – and market – the new sounds. However, social segregation meant that integrated audiences were either illegal or unlikely. But, greater profits could be made by selling records or performing to the wealthier white listeners than the poorer black audiences.

Ike Turner could see this; he had brains, guts, and ambition, but he needed a star to really push the Kings of Rhythm into the big time. And even better, he needed a star who would appeal to black and white audiences alike.

On the sidelines

None of this meant anything to Anna Mae, sitting at the bar of the Club Manhattan for her first night out. But the attention Ike Turner got right from his entrance interested Anna Mae. Ike cut a trim figure in his suit and tie. "When he got closer, I thought, 'God, he's ugly.' But there was something about him. Then he got up on stage and picked up his guitar. He hit one note and I thought, 'Jesus, listen to this guy play.' And that joint started rocking." The power of live music moves people. Anna Mae was hooked.

She begged Gene to see if Ike would let her sing. After all, girls less gifted than she were grabbing the microphone and joining in for a song. Anna Mae didn't know that when Gene had planted her at a

"The true roots for black gospel and spirituals can be traced to the extraordinary collision of cultures that took place at the beginning of the eighteenth century, as bonded African slave met the first flood of English Church hymns on American soil."

From Black Gospel – An illustrated History of the Gospel Sound.

stage-side table to keep an eye on her, he had told the saxophone player to drop a microphone nearby to pick up her humming and singing during the sets, or groups of songs. When Gene finally did ask Ike if he would give Anna Mae a chance on stage, Ike said sure, but never called her up.

A natural

At seventeen, Anna Mae Bullock was hardly a glamorous young trendsetter. She could sing, but she knew more about country walks, cleaning the house, and cheerleading than she did about night clubs. If there was one thing she wasn't, it was a swinger. She was still going to school, working harder playing basketball and being in school plays than at her studies, and expecting to graduate to a career in nursing. Any dreams of performing before crowds of people, of entertaining with her singing and dancing, seemed simply that: dreams.

Under Ike's supervision, Tina learned to sing new sounds, learning to wail and scream. Ike realized that Tina Turner had something special and that her voice and power were the key to success.

One night, between sets, Gene teased Alline with a microphone while Ike was on stage playing the piano. Anna Mae snatched the microphone from him and started singing along, "Darling, you know I love you . . . ." Later she remembered, "I just let loose, and everybody came running to see who it was."

The audience was overwhelmed. Ike called her to the stage to play an impromptu set, saying, "Giiirrrlll! I didn't know you could really sing!" By all accounts, that night saw a star being born. Ike introduced her to Club Manhattan as "Little Ann."

"Where I grew up it was all radio and church. What did I know about music? Here was Ike with his diamonds, suits, pink Cadillac, big house in East St. Louis, considered a rich black man, compared to where I was coming from. When he invited me to sing with him, oh, I was thrilled."

Ike Turner, however, had quite a dangerous reputation in St. Louis and Anna Mae did not want her mother, Zelma, to find out that she was sharing a

"Hearing Tina on slow, emotional tearjerkers, is just as exciting as listening to her blitz through an uptight, highspeed soul stomper. She's like a pilot carrying out an aerobic display, wings flashing, engine screaming."
Chris Welch, from
Take You Higher;
The Tina Turner Experience.

"We would pull up at the club, and I would get out and walk in and sit there real grand, like I was the star. And after a while, Ike would call me on stage. He'd say, 'Now we're gonna bring Little Ann up.' And I'd walk up there and sing my three songs, and everybody would clap. It was wonderful. They were clapping for me. Little Ann."

Tina Turner.

stage with him. But any secret like that is sure to make its way out. Zelma recalled how a lady dropped by one summer afternoon when Anna Mae had gone out swimming with some friends. The stranger said that Anna Mae was late for rehearsal. Zelma "hit the roof." While Anna Mae didn't feel she had done anything wrong, sneaking behind her mother's back to join the Kings of Rhythm, she also knew she would have to stop.

Setback

Zelma knew how difficult surviving as an African American woman could be. She expected Anna to finish high school and learn a trade like nursing. Although the United States was the so-called "Land of Opportunity," in the 1950s, women, especially black women, could expect more obstacles than options. Even if Anna Mae were luckier in marriage than Zelma had been, she would need job skills to carry her through. Singing might be fun, but Zelma did not feel that music was something Anna Mae could make a living from. Still, Zelma's refusal to take her daughter's aspirations seriously was crushing. "I just wanted to sing and dance so bad and I loved Ike's band. His music was what my physical energy was. Whenever I heard that music, I was dancing," Tina recalled.

If no amount of convincing would sway Zelma Bullock, then her daughter would just wait. Such patience and determination would serve Anna Mae throughout her life.

Breakthrough

The chance to sing, however, came a second time, thanks to Ike. Ike missed Anna Mae's contributions to the Club Manhattan gigs, so he decided to visit Zelma Bullock. He chose his outfit carefully, wearing smart clothes and adopting the polished manners that he had learned as a preacher's son. He asked Zelma's permission for Anna Mae to join the band for an important concert at a college, promising to supervise her every move.

Ike won Zelma's confidence and she finally agreed to allow Anna Mae to go. "Boy, was I happy! From then on, Ike and I were like brother and sister," Tina remembered. "He went out and bought me my first stage clothes: sequined dresses, honey, in pink and silver and blue, with long gloves up to here and rings to wear over them. Bare-backed shoes, stockings with seams, even a fur stole. Boy, I was sharp!

"I wasn't really making any money or anything, but still, just to be able to do something like that – wearing these clothes and standing up there singing with this band – I thought I had died and gone to heaven." Eventually, it was agreed that Anna Mae could join the band regularly, but this heaven only

Ike looks on as he and his guitar keep the beat for the female vocals. Tina Turner shares the stage with the Ikettes, the singing-dancing-prancing backup for the Ike and Tina Turner Revue.

lasted from Friday night until Sunday. Every Monday morning Anna Mae was expected to be fresh and ready for school.

"Her voice combined the emotional force of a great blues singer with a sheer, wallpaper-peeling power that seemed made-to-order for the age of amplification," coauthor of Tina's autobiography, Kurt Loder, recalled. Drummer Gene Washington said, "Her voice was different for the type of music we were doing. A woman doing that type of thing then was kind of a no-no. . . . So Anna Mae was something completely different for us – but she fit right in. And things just exploded right from there."

Romance and responsibility

In the whirlwind of her new weekend work, Anna Mae met a saxophone player with the Kings of Rhythm, Raymond Hill. He was quieter and more thoughtful than the other band members. Without any formal education, Raymond had trained himself to play music with a passion and intensity that attracted Anna Mae.

The band all lived together in Ike's house in East St. Louis. Here they rehearsed night and day – whenever Ike could find the time between the endless gigs. When she wasn't at home or going to school, Anna Mae would be there too. It was easy to socialize when they weren't rehearsing. Romance bloomed between Raymond and Anna Mae.

At eighteen, Anna Mae learned that she was pregnant and Zelma asked her to leave the family home. She moved into Ike's house for a while, but continued going to school. "It was bad enough that I was pregnant," she said. "I had to finish school or my mother would have gone crazy." She and Raymond talked about marriage, but made no definite plans. Then Raymond injured his ankle. Thinking it was a sprain, he played on for two nights. Soon he was in the hospital. From there, he went back to his home town in Mississippi to recover.

Anna Mae was now on her own, living in the house with Ike and the rest of the band, and the odds were against her. Still in her teens, she faced the challenge of raising a child by herself. In the 1950s young women weren't expected to embark on motherhood without a husband.

Jealousy

Meanwhile, Ike's common-law wife, Lorraine Taylor, was also in the house. It was a fiery relationship, with Lorraine struggling to cope with Ike's ambitions and his adoring fans. She believed

"In the very beginning, Ike and I really were just like brother and sister. I wasn't his type of woman, and he wasn't my type of man, either. But we communicated through music. I loved what he played. And I could sing his ideas.

Tina Turner.

that Ike had affairs with other women. When Anna Mae entered the band scene, Lorraine grew very suspicious.

She saw that Anna Mae's singing talents held promise for Ike's future. Lorraine supposed that Anna Mae knew her own value, and that she was after Ike. Ike had already showered Anna Mae with clothes and jewels and Lorraine knew that such gifts could buy not only loyalty, but love.

Desperate acts

When Raymond had left and Anna Mae showed signs of being pregnant, Lorraine lost all perspective. She took a pistol and a poker from the stove and crept in on a sleeping Anna Mae. "I woke up and there was Lorraine, with the gun and the poking iron. I guess she was going to beat me until I told her the truth and then shoot me. But I really hadn't done anything wrong at that time." There was nothing to tell, and Lorraine gave up threatening Anna Mae.

Sadly, Lorraine then walked to the bathroom to turn the gun on herself. Lorraine shot herself in the chest. In the hospital, she blamed Ike for injuring her. The rantings were attributed to delirium. Lorraine recovered. In October, 1958, she gave birth to a son, whom she and Ike named Ike Jr.

Motherhood

In the light of the difficult situation in Ike's house and all the tensions surrounding Lorraine's suicide attempt, Anna Mae moved back to live with her mother. She graduated in the spring of 1958 and on August 20, her son, Raymond Craig, was born. Zelma did not welcome the baby into her home, so Anna Mae struck out on her own. She and baby Craig rented a small apartment in an area crawling with juke joints and streetwalking prostitutes.

Meanwhile, Anna Mae's role in the band expanded. She was now earning $15 a week singing with the

Ike Turner. Ike always had a talent for music and high ambition to go with it. He formed his band, Kings of Rhythm, while he was still going to school. He was a great musician, playing the piano and guitar. However, he was looking for a vocalist who would guarantee his route to stardom.

The Ike and Tina Turner Revue was formed after the success of the single "A Fool in Love," which featured Anna Mae as the lead singer.

Kings of Rhythm. She added to this with a day job as a nurse's assistant at nearby Barnes Hospital.

Conveniently for the young mother, Anna Mae was assigned to the maternity ward. Barnes served a wealthy clientele and one patient caught Anna Mae's attention because she looked so pretty and happy, even after having just given birth. Anna Mae knew what a physical drain having a baby was and she was amazed at the woman's composure and good looks. She asked the woman for some tips and was shown an eye pencil and mascara. "While she was there, I sort of started to pattern myself after her a bit. I went out that weekend and bought the Maybelline pencil and the mascara, and that was the beginning of makeup for me."

Despite such perks, the day job proved too much to balance with the heavy demands on Anna Mae. Soon, she and her baby left their small apartment and moved in with Ike and the band.

The first thing Ike did was to raise Anna Mae's salary to $25 a week! Ike was becoming Anna Mae's protector and provider on a full-time basis. Yet nothing comes without a price, and Ike demanded excellence and absolute loyalty. Looking back, Tina

Turner saw that as the turning point. "And that was the beginning, although I didn't know it at the time, of Ike Turner moving in on my life." There would be no turning back.

A Fool in Love

Anna Mae was now one of the main singers for the Kings of Rhythm and she was also in Ike's house permanently. Lorraine and Ike had a second son, named Michael, but their relationship remained uneven. Ike seemed to always be in the company of other women. Ike and Lorraine split up for a time, and Ike and Anna Mae became lovers. But Ike and Lorraine's separation had not ended formally. Just when Anna Mae found out that she and Ike had conceived a child, Lorraine moved back into the house.

Ike continued his relationship with Anna Mae, and she continued to work constantly as she carried their child. But, after a while, Anna Mae left the band's house once again, with Craig in tow, and found herself another apartment.

Grabbing an opportunity

In the spring of 1960, the Kings of Rhythm were preparing to cut, or record, a new single called "A Fool in Love." Ike had struck upon the idea of having female backup singers behind the main voice, and he set about selecting them. The song would feature a regular member of the Kings of Rhythm, Art Lassiter. Lassiter, however, like other members before him, was having a difficult time getting along with Ike. They had argued about money, and Art chose the recording session to let Ike know what he thought about Ike's ways. With the studio rented and the musicians ready, Lassiter failed to show up: Ike was left without a lead singer.

Ike Turner managed to get out of that bind. He had just caught on to the technology of multi-track recordings, where instruments and vocalists are recorded separately. A complete sound can be engineered by adjusting the volume and contribution of the individual tracks. Track recording allows the

The song that sent Tina to the charts proved an apt description for the girl herself. What began as a friendship turned into a relationship between Ike and his young protégée. For music fans, the single hit turned Ike and Tina Turner into a sensation.

25

studio engineer to assume the role once held by the band leader or conductor, blending and balancing the contributions of the different musicians to create the finished sound.

Ike asked Anna Mae to join the band at the studio. Then he recorded her voice on a separate track from all the others. Ike planned to erase Anna Mae's voice and replace it with Art Lassiter's, when Lassiter finally showed up,

But once Anna Mae's voice hit the vinyl, Ike had little use for Art Lassiter. He played the record for the crowds at the Club Manhattan and they went wild. He sent demo tapes, or rough versions of the

This page and opposite: In denim or sequins, Tina's earthy elegance always captures the eye.
According to one of her biographers, Steven Ivory, "Turner is the embodiment of the rock and roll she so valiantly sings."

song, to independent recording companies around the country in the hope of getting a recording deal.

One tape made its way to the manager of Sue Records in New York City, Juggy Murray. Murray didn't know Ike "from a hole in the wall when the tape arrived in my office. But I knew it was a hit." Ike was surprised and thrilled by Murray's enthusiasm. As Murray put it, "Ike was a musical genius, but he wouldn't know a hit record if it fell off the Empire State Building and hit him on the head." After all, Ike hadn't had much faith in Anna Mae's contribution, but that was the sound that Sue Records wanted to sell. For Sue Records, Anna Mae was "A Fool in Love."

Juggy Murray presented Ike Turner with a recording contract and offered him a $25,000 advance, which in 1960 was a large sum. In return, Murray expected that Turner would seize the moment and capitalize on the sizzling voice of his new lead singer. Ike agreed. He started planning a revue built around his guitar playing and musical direction, plus Anna Mae's voice.

Name game

Ike planned to produce and manage the group, choreograph the revue, and either write or arrange all the songs. Ike also decided to release the single under a new name: Ike and Tina Turner.

At twenty-one, Anna Mae Bullock became Tina Turner overnight, without being consulted or even warned. Ike was busy inventing a new image for Anna, one that made the most of her powerful voice

and wild dancing. As a boy, Ike had loved jungle movies with scantily clad actresses roaming through the trees with the apes, and they all had exotic names like Nyoka and Sheena. Tina Turner would be Ike's wild woman.

What's in a name?

One of the band members remembered Ike's search for the new name and his reasoning behind it – Ike "wanted to change Anna Mae to Tina to safeguard his own control over the situation. He gave her his name, and there's no way she would have stuck it as long as she did otherwise. If she'd had her own name

Bottom right: After the hit with "A Fool in Love," Ike got the taste of success. Here, surrounded by his singers, he seemed the king of a sequined mountain and he was reluctant to let it go. The Ike and Tina Turner Revue followed their first hit with a string of others, such as "It's Gonna Work Out Fine," "Poor Fool" and "I Idolize You." All of these reached the Top 10 in the R & B charts in the United States.

there wouldn't have been a thing Ike could have done about anything, legally. So he was thinking ahead when he gave her that name."

Ike had learned that if he wanted to reap the rewards, he had to keep his own name on everything. Now with the Sue Record contract sewn up, those assets included Anna Mae. It seemed as though Ike would stop at nothing to secure their future.

With Tina pregnant, Ike thought he was making his big break, and Tina was thinking hard about Ike's big plans. "I went to talk to him," she recounted. "First, he told me how it was going to be from then on: he would pay my rent, but basically keep all the money for himself. I told him I didn't want to get involved any further with him. And that was the first time he beat me up. With a shoe stretcher. . . ."

"A Fool in Love" swept the nation. It was the record Ike had been praying for. The single had "legs," a term used in the music industry to mean that a record had staying power. It flew to the No. 2 position in the R & B charts, and even showed impressively at No. 27 in the rock charts in the United States. For a song like this, that was success indeed. It appealed to black listeners raised on rhythm and blues and to white youth hungry for rock and roll, a "crossover" hit.

Crossover is the industry's term for a song that is aimed at a certain audience, but which gains acceptance in the wider population. A success with

black audiences promised only limited profits. True success meant reaching black and white, across the board. After this first crossover hit, Ike increasingly sought songs that would have wide appeal.

Who needs who?

Ike was determined to mastermind the success of the band, under the banner of the Ike and Tina Turner Revue. He was equally determined to control its profits. With a young child and another on the way, Tina was trapped. The Revue played as many as eighteen performances each week, earning $450 for every show, but Tina never saw a dime.

Ike needed a woman who would devote herself to his dreams, a woman who would work selflessly in pursuit of his ideals. Ike knew music. He was learning all there was to know about the business. Tina, on the other hand, was pure, raw talent. She needed a teacher and a director to shape her style. Tina needed a manager to arrange the gigs and get more recording contracts. That's how the music business works.

Tina had trusted Ike. In those days, women were raised to look to men for guidance and recognition of their own achievements, sacrificing their own needs to their partner's opinions. Tina was a quick learner and always professional, but Ike was slow to notice that. He expected to lead and, likewise, expected her to follow. As she strove for professional acceptance and excellence, Tina found herself going from prodigy to employee to slave. All the promise in Tina's future was laced with pain. Passion and determination sustained Tina through her struggle for a voice of her own.

The Ike and Tina Turner Revue

That same year Anna Mae, now named Tina, was hospitalized with jaundice. She was still pregnant with Ike's child. Despite her condition, Ike decided it was time to start touring with the band and literally kidnapped Tina from her bed. This time, he was sure they would be heading for the big time.

Opposite right: Angela Bassett portrays the long-suffering Tina Turner in the movie What's Love Got to Do With It? *Actor Larry Fishburne (below) plays the turbulent Ike Turner.*

To start the ball rolling they played small clubs and college parties throughout the southern states of America. But the band, with Ike at the helm, was ready to make a bid for better clubs and bigger crowds.

On this "Fool in Love" tour, the Revue made it all the way to the Apollo Theater, a celebrated hot spot in New York City's Harlem district. On that star-studded night at the Apollo, Tina won the audience over. Eight months pregnant, she amazed the Apollo crowd by jumping from the stage into the audience. Just as "A Fool in Love" was peaking on the pop charts, Ike and Tina started to play on live television shows that broadcast the Revue into living rooms across the country.

A family of four

There was no looking back to St. Louis now. Tina Turner was preparing to give birth to their child and Ike decided now was the time to make the big move to Los Angeles. Los Angeles was a thriving place for African American culture and almost one-third of the independent recording companies were based there. If Tina was going to be tied down with caring for the new baby, Ike wanted to make sure of his chances of finding work.

On October 27, 1960, Tina gave birth to Ike's child, Ronald Renelle. Ike's common-law wife and mother of two of his sons, Lorraine, drove Tina to the hospital. The baby was the spitting image of Ike. Soon the love triangle became unbearable. Lorraine left Ike and their sons Ike Jr. and Michael. So Ike and Tina started living as a family with all four boys – Ike Jr., Michael, Craig, and Ronald Renelle – growing up as brothers. In 1962, when Tina was twenty-three, she and Ike drove to Mexico for an improvised wedding.

The duo depended on one another. Tina remembers, "I would have been lost in my life at that point without him [Ike]. I mean, I could do two things: work in a hospital or sing with Ike's band. I didn't know anything else. Or anybody else. And I wanted to sing."

Dance fever

Just as the Turners were settling down as a family, the rest of the nation was jumping to its feet.

The 1960s ushered in a dance craze. The Ike and

Tina Turner Revue was ready to jump on the bandwagon – and grab the reins! What started with "The Twist" was followed by a score of toe-tapping, hip-shaking moves that put America's young people on their feet and having fun. No one could boogie, though, like the frenzied Tina Turner.

The success of the group with Tina and a female backup made Ike decide to give the new idea a try, using the name "Ikettes." Three Ikettes plus Tina made four flying, gyrating bodies.

Tina rehearsed the Ikettes endlessly, before and after shows, making sure that each new dance was polished to perfection. Her discipline and enthusiasm for the dances inspired the Ikettes, dissolving their constant fatigue from touring. Thanks to Tina, such polish and shine gave the Revue a professional image. They worked like a well-oiled machine, with Tina performing in overdrive.

Tina created routines that her audiences could pick up and dance themselves. "The way I dance is the way I feel. I choreographed all my own dances, and

Los Angeles, the city of big dreams or deep disappointments. The city holds the entertainment paradise of Hollywood in its suburbs. Actors, singers, all types of performers, try their luck in L.A. hoping for the big break. Ike felt that the Revue had to move to the city in order to establish a name for itself.

they are all simple. The audience aren't dancers. They want to feel that they can do what I'm doing." Tina was conscious of the public image that she was creating. As black performers, she felt that she and the Ikettes were branded as sexually provocative

Appearing on the sixties British music show, Ready Steady Go. *Such in-studio performances by the Revue were televised to households across the United States and Britain. These clinical studios were a far cry from the smoky night clubs that were more familiar to the band, but prime time TV coverage was a great way to pursue success.*

dancers. But, Tina insisted, "We do a clean show. They used to call it 'wild.' Now they call it 'energy,' and it's acceptable."

The look

The Revue itself was arranged like a lively religious meeting. The band, numbering up to nine members, warmed up the audience with instrumental numbers. Ike often showed off his extraordinary musicianship on the electric guitar. Band members and each Ikette would take the stage for a solo. When the audience was good and ready for Tina Turner, she would step on stage and sing her heart out. The Ikettes behind her became her congregation, echoing and clapping as she sung her message out to the hearts and minds of the enchanted fans. The fever pitch of the performances brought the house down – at least twice a night, nearly three hundred nights a year!

The way Tina Turner and the Ikettes looked helped to give the Revue an energetic, high-speed

"He [Ike Turner] is not just a cool presence, but an electrifying one, capable of charm, and also frightening."

Jay Carr, *from the* Boston Globe, *June 1993.*

feel. An over-enthusiastic bleach job had damaged Tina's hair, but Tina was not one to be defeated by details. To cover the mess, she donned a wig. It was then the fashion for African Americans to straighten the natural kinks in their hair, using gels and hot irons. The wigs that Tina and the Ikettes adopted were made of long, straight black hair. When they danced, the hair flew up, beating the air and adding to the extraordinary commotion.

Tina's solution proved pure genius. Even when natural hair came into fashion with the "Afro," a unisex style where hair was teased apart and left to stand like a halo around the head, Tina Turner and the Ikettes stuck with the long, pressed look.

What changed the most was the length of their skirts. As the decade progressed, the miniskirt ruled. As standards relaxed, more women performers were welcomed into the limelight with short, short skirts.

Hard knocks

But there was a secret that was hidden from the spotlights – bruises that regularly stained Tina's beauty. Tina was often forced to mask her black eyes behind sunglasses, and coat her bruises and split lips with makeup. The suspected beatings were sometimes so extreme that she had difficulty speaking properly, yet she was still expected to sing. It was now Tina's turn, like Lorraine before her, to believe that Ike was having affairs. He even invited other women into their family home.

The Ike and Tina Turner Revue had a smattering of hits in the sixties. They were working steadily – to exhaustion, but they never found the song to get them through the ceiling that was placed on so many African American artists.

In 1966, Ike was approached by Phil Spector, a boy-genius who, at twenty-five, had changed the sound of rock and roll. Although he approached Ike, he was actually interested in Tina. Spector knew that as her manager, producer, boss and husband, Ike was the only route to reach Tina.

Spector had pioneered a technique of layering orchestral sounds to create a blend of melody and

Musical producer Phil Spector looks out gravely from behind an electronic sound board. Spector had a great head for business and was in charge of a record company, making him a millionaire by the age of twenty-one. In the creation of his "wall of sound," Spector spent money enough for five albums to cut the single "River Deep, Mountain High" with Tina Turner.

33

echo that went at its listeners with the force of a diesel truck. He now had a new single, which promised the most dramatic use ever of his celebrated "wall of sound," and he needed a singer. It would take a gutsy vocalist to match Spector's sound.

"River deep, Mountain High"

Spector had seen the Ike and Tina Turner Revue in Hollywood and was entranced by Tina's vocal power. His orchestration for "River Deep, Mountain High" was ready, and Spector was sure he had found the voice he was looking for.

Spector offered Ike about $20,000 to allow Tina Turner to perform. The deal specified one important rule, however: Ike was not invited to perform, or even appear at the studio for the weeks that Tina

When making a record, sound levels can be changed and tracks, or a specific section of the record, can be remixed. A number of takes of the same song are usually recorded and the best result used. But once the tracks are set and the record pressed, the sounds are there to stay. Patience, technical know-how, and creative vision are needed to make a saleable sound.

rehearsed the song. Ike agreed, on the condition that the song would still be released under the name of "Ike and Tina Turner" even though it was Tina's piece. Tina had no say in the matter, and it was a deal.

That recording session changed Tina's life. For the first time she felt like a professional artist, in control of her own instrument, her voice. After years of singing exactly as Ike instructed, Tina was free to explore singing as an expression of herself. Spector wasn't interested in the screaming and wailing she had perfected for Ike. Spector's respect and love for

Tina's voice affected her deeply. Learning the melody "was like carving furniture." Performing the song with the wall of sound was an ecstatic explosion. Record producer Bob Krasnow remembered his hair standing on end, "It was like the whole room exploded. I'll never forget that as long as I live, man. It was a magic moment." The song proved Tina was an artist in her own right, without Ike.

Tina Turner and Mick Jagger, of the Rolling Stones, shimmy together at the Live Aid benefit concert in 1985. Their friendship provided Tina with strength and encouragement as she built her solo career.

Across the sea

Surprisingly, "River Deep, Mountain High" was not as successful in the United States as had been hoped. The song did not fit into the simple music categories that the radio stations relied on. It made it to No. 28 in the rock charts in its first week out, but didn't manage to climb any higher.

However, the song made its way across the Atlantic, where it created great waves. It spent thirteen weeks in the Top 50 of the British charts, shooting as high as No. 3. British radio stations did not categorize music so specifically. A record didn't have to be R & B or rock, for example, before it would be played. Each record was judged on its own merits – if it sounded good, it was played.

The tremendous reception brought an invaluable invitation: for Tina to open for the Rolling Stones 1966 tour. After that first tour, the admiration and affection that Tina and the Stones shared saw Tina through her hard times ahead. It was Tina who taught Mick Jagger the "pony," and Jagger would often be found watching and dancing about in the wings as the Revue danced up a storm out on stage.

All alone

The emotional and physical demands being made on Tina Turner were wearing her out. In her isolation, Tina had found a sympathetic camaraderie with the Ikettes who offered her money to help her to escape from Ike. But each time she had left, Ike had brought her back. And although in her heart she knew there was a way out, Tina Turner could not see it yet.

Domestic violence is only too great a reality for thousands of families. Wife-beating is a common form of violence, but children, men, and the elderly are also terrorized by physical violence or the threat of violence. It's hard to say what makes some people act in this way.

Tina was raising the four Turner boys. She felt she was dependent on Ike, not only because he was the children's father, but because he was her employer – her means to earning a living. Also, as Ike's fortunes grew, he helped support Tina's mother and sister, Zelma and Alline. This left Tina with no one beyond his control to turn to. All Tina knew was the band and the road.

In 1968, desperate for escape, Tina, now twenty-nine, attempted suicide. She poisoned herself with a bottle of sleeping pills before a performance and was rushed to the hospital, where her stomach was pumped. For someone with such vitality to tempt death shows the depth of the Turner tragedy.

Dry spell

The 1970s saw things slowing down for Ike and Tina. There had been some record successes and lots of chances to appear on television and in movies. Now the R & B sounds that Ike loved were being marketed under the name of "soul." Yet, caught as he was between rock and soul, Ike's imagination was no longer coming up with great songs. Tina was often having to finish Ike's half-written work.

Ike's creativity was drying up and Tina worked overtime to hold the band together. She suggested they cover, or record, songs by other groups. Their renditions of the Beatles' song "Come Together" and the Rolling Stones' "Honky Tonk Women" were stunning for their raw energy. A smooth song, "Proud Mary," recorded by a band called Creedence Clearwater Revival became an exciting adventure with Tina at the front.

By this time, Tina's love for Ike had been exhausted – it seemed as though it was always Tina making the sacrifices. Ike was unwilling to rethink his plans or compromise his ambitions. He had

"I have learned that success is to be measured not so much by the position that one has reached in life as by the obstacles which one has overcome while trying to succeed."

Booker T. Washington.

achieved a sizable wealth. He spent hundreds of thousands of dollars building an elaborate recording studio so that he could work day and night to concoct the sound that would make him the king of the music scene. Ike never succeeded.

The 1973 song "Nutbush City Limits" was the last Top 30 hit Ike and Tina would ever make together. It was written by Tina about growing up in Tennessee. "Nutbush City Limits" grew from her heart, voicing her memories of a time long before Ike came into her life.

Cracking up

Ike Turner's downfall was drugs. Ike tried cocaine and could not give it up. Cocaine is a substance derived from the leaves of the South

Nathan Schulsinger worked in the emergency room of the Daniel Freeman Hospital in Inglewood, Los Angeles. He reported on Tina's visits as he remembered them, "She would come in, in pretty bad shape, all beat-up and bruised, face swollen, bloody nose . . . eyes all puffed out and black." Makeup and dark glasses would hide her wounds when she went back out on stage.

American shrub, coca. Cocaine is a powerful and addictive drug that has an incredibly dangerous effect on the brain. The overpowering sense of energy produced by cocaine leads to a savage craving for more of the drug. This craving, or addiction, is hard to break once it has taken hold.

Ike, who in his early days had forbidden the Kings of Rhythm to drink alcohol in his presence, had walked into cocaine's trap. Under its influence, he seemed to grow more intolerant and unreasonable. Tina's son, Craig, reported that Ike would sometimes snap so fast that he seemed out of his mind.

In order to keep the Revue on track and take control of the situation, Tina adopted a more active role. "Ike was so desperate for a hit and I wanted him to have one, too. I was doing everything I could – touring with him, staying up all night in the studio with him. . . . And now I was even writing songs. But it was never enough." When Ike asked Tina what she had ever given him, she stood up for herself. It was an important first step to setting the record straight.

As she entered her thirties, with the boys growing into teenagers, Tina started surveying her life. She

Tina, played by Angela Bassett, comforts Ike, played by Larry Fishburne, in a tender moment during the film What's Love Got to Do With It? *In real life, Tina's loyalty to Ike was no act. Even when Ike was deserted by the rest of his band members, Tina stood by him.*

Tina and Ike pictured with their sons. From the left, Ike's sons by Lorraine Taylor, Ike Jr. (standing) and Michael (seated) with Tina's sons, Craig and Ronnie, on the right. Tina raised all the boys as her own.

regarded the years of work, recording and touring on the road, as Ike's career, ". . . it was Ike's songs, mostly, and they were always about Ike's life – and I had to sing them. I was just his tool." Tina had pledged her loyalty to Ike, promising to stick by him when other band members had come and gone. But his descent into drugs and all that came with it was not a path that Tina could tread.

Unable to discuss their difficulties openly, Tina began to write letters to Ike to express her feelings. Each time he read a letter, she ended up with a black eye. "My left eye pretty much stayed black, and my nose was always swollen," she remembered. It was a frightening and an unsettling time. The boys, growing fast into men themselves, were afraid and confused.

Below and right: "I knew I needed something to help me deal with what my life had become, to help me find a way out. . . ." Tina discovered an inner world of peace and beauty through her Buddhist chants and meditation. In the Buddhist tradition, Butsadan is the name for the cabinet that contains life's necessities. Inside are a candle, incense, water, fruit, and a scroll of sacred writing. The items help the person to focus on meditation.

One of Ike's secretaries introduced Tina to Buddhist chanting. Chanting, a form of worship in several of the world's religions, is the repetitive singing of a sound or phrase. It relaxes the body and clears the mind. Tina was charmed by its cleansing effects and began to chant regularly. Chanting introduced her to the whole Buddhist religion and the richness of traditions that were far removed from her own life in Los Angeles. Through Buddhism, she became convinced that there was an end to her pain and torment.

Take control

Tina's wish for independence was answered, slowly. The first break came in 1974 when she was invited to read for a role in a movie called *Tommy*. It was a movie based on a rock opera by the British band The

Who. It had been a hard choice between David Bowie and Tina Turner, but for the role of the wicked Acid Queen the producers wanted the raucous electricity of Tina's "wild woman" image.

There were many stars packed into the film, including the American actor Jack Nicholson and the British musician Elton John. Tina's was a small role, but critics hailed her performance as one of the best in the wacky film. Said one critic, "Tina threw herself into the role, singing with tremulous, lip-quivering power. . . . The effect on the audience was

When watching her power-packed performances, it's hard to imagine anyone holding Tina down. Tina was delighted with her role as the Acid Queen in the movie Tommy. *Ike seemed frightened of Tina's personal power, but Tina was intent on discovering her independence and inner strength.*

startling." For Tina, it meant another international success without Ike.

Tina's self-confidence was growing stronger as she proved herself again and again to be an able professional performer and a caring mother. Still, the final parting from Ike came as a surprise even to Tina herself.

No turning back

In 1976 Tina, Ike, and the band set out for the start of a big U.S. tour. The first flight took them to Texas. Ike hadn't had any sleep for five days. In the airport

"I will prepare and some day my chance will come."
Abraham Lincoln.

*Tina salutes her audience.
Identifying with her
audiences was part of the
secret of Tina's success. "I
think people see that I'm
not one of those Hollywood
stars who lies back with my
silks and chiffons on,
treating people like
peasants. I didn't want to
be a victim of Hollywood,
so I decided to stay with
the people. I think that's
why they welcomed me
back so quickly."*

limousine, Tina refused to hold a piece of sticky chocolate melting in the heat. This made Ike angry.

For the first time, Tina, now thirty-six, stood up for herself. Trading punches, Tina screamed at Ike the way she had heard him yell for years.

The Turners entered their hotel bloody and swollen. Once Tina was sure that Ike had drifted off to sleep she left, not stopping to collect any belongings. Fearing discovery by Ike or his assistants, she hid in an alley. Several hours later, she limped away until she came to another hotel. She entered, still stained with blood, and asked the manager for help.

She had only thirty-six cents in her pocket. She had no safe way to get back to Los Angeles and no money of her own at home. But at least she was away from Ike.

From this day forth, there would be no turning back for Tina Turner.

A little help from her friends

Tina telephoned Ike's lawyer, who sent Tina money and a plane ticket to return to Los Angeles.

Tina Turner was forced to move from house to house, as her friends and guardians were threatened by Ike. The concert tour was ruined and Ike wasn't the only one who was angry.

After a calm conversation, during which Tina made it clear that the marriage and the musical partnership were both over, Ike sent all four teenage boys to stay with Tina. She had been surviving by cleaning people's houses, and was not prepared for the additional responsibility of the boys. But sending them back to Ike, who was spending all his time locked up in his studio and, she believed, drugged on cocaine, would have been a worse option. Tina was forced to support the boys on whatever money she could earn and on government food stamps.

Clearly it was time for Tina Turner to get back to doing the thing she did best: performing.

Tina started appearing on television game shows and sitcoms. Slowly, Tina and the boys adjusted to their new, modest lifestyle. The boys occasionally saw their father. Ike continued to threaten the whole

*"Tina Turner now gives
the signals and calls the
shots. Ike and the extra-
long guitar cord are gone;
so are the horn section
and the Ikettes. Only Tina
remains: bigger, more
beautiful, and more loved
than ever before. Her time
has come."*

Ron Wynn, from Tina; The Tina
Turner Story.

42

family. Now, however, Tina was in the driver's seat and getting ready to hit the road. Tina Turner was driving herself all the way to the top!

Showtime

Her first job was assembling a band and lining up some performance dates. These were tricky to arrange for two reasons. First, Tina was known in the music industry as the second half of "Ike and Tina Turner," and few people were ready to recognize that Tina was a worthy and exciting artist in her own right. What's more, the Turners' reputation had been badly stained when the tour of the summer of 1976 had to be abandoned, and Tina had left the act in the lurch. Tina Turner had a lot to prove by striking out as a solo act.

It was exciting to mount the show. Tina was good at choreography and costuming, and her stepson Ike Jr. was ready to engineer the sound. With years of performing under her belt, she had no problem finding material. In addition to old Revue songs like "River Deep" and "Proud Mary," Tina played some cabaret numbers.

Her audiences were no longer the hip African Americans raised on R & B, or the rocking white youth hungry for rock and roll. Tina was preparing to play Las Vegas, where she would have to provide

Las Vegas is a city of neon lights and casinos glittering in the middle of the Nevada desert, in the United States. Show biz meets gambling at the city's numerous luxury hotels. For Tina, Vegas was the first stop on a road that would lead to international fame.

Now it was Tina's turn to decide how long – or short – her hemline would be! The uniform appearance of the Ikettes was replaced by a fresh originality. For the new Tina, top-quality, precision performances were a high priority in order to re-establish her career.

glitz, high kicks, and a slick, good time. Her new show was well-received, but the music industry didn't know if it was a fresh start or a slow fizzle out.

Keeping the name

Ike's menacing antics and his pleas for Tina's return continued, even as Tina undertook divorce proceedings. In order to tie up the arrangements as quickly as possible, Tina did not contest any of Ike's claims to their shared property. When she said goodbye to Ike, she left behind her home, her belongings, her income from their records, and her shares in the recording studio that she had helped to have built.

The one thing she refused to part with, however, was her name. Ike may have christened her Tina Turner, but she was the source of the charisma and

"The best things in life are yours, if you can appreciate yourself."
Dale Carnegie.

Giving it all she's got. Tina Turner ensures that the crowd at her concert in Honolulu receive her best efforts.

power attached to the image. Her stage name was too precious to let go. Besides, too much had happened since her girlhood in Nut Bush, for her ever to return as Anna Mae Bullock.

Despite her compromises, Tina was still left to pay the bill for the tour that she had deserted. Concert producers and promoters were not interested in marital problems when there were profits at stake. Not only was each venue suing for a return of the advance that they had paid, but they also expected additional sums as damages. With their fans and followings, the venues had reputations on the line as well. It took Tina Turner, now in her late thirties, eight years of constant hard work to pay off this debt. She regularly left the stage triumphant after an exhilarating show only to find debt collectors waiting by her dressing room door. Yet Tina Turner was the last to speak bitterly or look back with regret. In her mind, the irritating debts were a small price to pay for a new lease of life.

Friends from far away

Things were looking up in 1979, when Tina was invited to be the special guest on pop star Olivia Newton-John's television special. Tina and Olivia were as opposite as could be – which made them a great pair in performance. After filming, Tina met Newton-John's ambitious manager, Lee Kramer. At forty, Tina Turner realized that what she needed to help her achieve the goals she set herself was a manager. She wasn't looking for a boss, but rather for a business partner.

Lee Kramer wasn't the man for her, but he knew who was. He introduced Tina to Roger Davies. Davies saw through the sequins and tuxedos in Tina's Las Vegas show to the promise within her that was waiting to be realized.

Davies was keen to get Tina off the cabaret circuit and back into New York. He fixed up a series of shows at the trendy New York club, the Ritz. Here, the audience was often full of celebrities. When the Rolling Stones came to New York for their 1981 U.S. tour, they saw Tina at the Ritz and then swooped her up to join them for their New York area concerts. Instead of just opening for the Stones as she and Ike had, Tina also shared the stage with Mick Jagger, for a duet of "Honky Tonk Women."

Tina became quite a regular at the Ritz. Before one

Below left: Few performers can match the hip-grinding Mick Jagger. When the two stars shared a stage it guaranteed an event to remember.

Below right: At the Rainforest Benefit Concert at Carnegie Hall, New York, 1993, Tina and the Canadian rock guitarist Bryan Adams enjoy a well-earned hug after their duet "It's only Love." Adams has turned down further offers for duets, saying, "it's a no-go because once you've sung with the queen who do you sing with?"

performance, she noticed Roger Davies was rushing round in a state of excitement. It wasn't until after the show that she realized why: all the executives from the record companies Capitol and EMI were in the audience. The show had been a great success. Tina Turner was making a name for herself.

London calling

The British music scene had changed a lot since Tina's first visit in the late 1960s. The rock of the Rolling Stones, Eric Clapton, and The Who was being challenged by the alarming sounds of punk.

In the confusion, a musicians' trade union was trying to quell the use of electronic synthesizers because the technology threatened to replace live players. To oppose this measure, two musicians, Martyn Ware and Ian Craig Marsh, known as part of the band Heaven 17, decided to record an album of pop greats – with electric synthesizers replacing bands. Their company B.E.F. invited Tina to sing a track on the forthcoming album, ironically called *Music of Quality and Distinction.*

Tina was not pleased to be singing "Ball of Confusion," an R & B song first made famous by the Temptations. But she flew to London after B.E.F. offered her $2,000 and plane tickets.

Tina Turner shares the microphone with Keith Richards (left) and Eric Clapton (right). Both were part of the revolution in modern rock music that drew Tina from her musical roots into a twentieth century legend.

Since she and Davies had come this far, they might as well try. The recording was made in just a day. The album was a hit in Britain, and Tina's rendition of the old standard showed that she had a style that blended her R & B roots with an awareness of eighties' rock. Tina Turner's gifts were finally allowing her to cross the boundaries of "soul" and "rock," black and white.

Private Dancer

The stage was now set for a triumphant comeback. Tina recorded a cover version of Al Green's "Let's Stay Together," and her soaring interpretation sent the song straight into the British charts and hearts.

The album Private Dancer *helped confirm the fact that Tina Turner was back. It reached the Top 10 in the album charts both the United States and Britain, holding its position there for over nine months. The album sold over ten million copies worldwide.*

When the song finally did see light in the United States, it entered the Top 40 and reached the height of No. 5 in the soul charts.

Now was the time when Tina Turner would either make it or break it. Unbelievably, her record company expected Tina to have all the songs for a new album within two weeks so they could get the record out quickly! Tina Turner had to hustle if she was to meet the deadline.

Word went out on the music scene in London and famous friends came running. Mark Knopfler of Dire Straits offered the song that became the haunting title track, "Private Dancer." On an earlier trip, Davies had bought every David Bowie cassette available

Previous page: Tina Turner was British pop star David Bowie's first choice for his duet "Tonight," recorded in 1984. Ten years earlier, Tina and Bowie were both on the casting short list for the role of the Acid Queen in The Who's rock opera Tommy. Bowie must have learned that if you can't beat her, get her to join you on stage!

Opposite: In 1986, Tina was invited by Los Angeles Mayor, Tom Bradley, to become the 1831st star on the Hollywood Walk of Fame. At the age of forty-seven, Tina Turner was proving that it's never too late to achieve your dream.

Below right: Tina joined Lionel Richie's national tour around the United States in 1984. When Richie and Turner met again to receive their Grammy Awards in February 1985, they were meeting as equals.

and knew that "1984" would sound exciting à la Tina. A friend of Davies's from Australia offered two compositions, "Show Some Respect" and "What's Love Got to Do With It?" The gem among them was a song written for Tina called "I Might Have Been Queen."

Soon the list was complete. The team went to work. They made their deadline. As the singles were released, Tina was touring the United States as a special guest of Lionel Richie's national tour. When the record hit the stores her old fans learned how much her voice had matured. Her performances had raw energy as well as hard-earned wisdom. In time, the album *Private Dancer* sold ten million copies.

Just as the Lionel Richie tour wound down, the song "What's Love Got to Do With It?" grabbed No. 1 on the U.S. charts for three weeks running. The very same day that her song hit the No. 1 spot, Tina signed a contract to co-star in a *Mad Max* movie starring Mel Gibson. Before it was released, Tina also appeared in the all-star recording "We Are the World" to benefit famine relief in Africa.

Just desserts

In February 1985, Tina Turner, at the age of forty-five, was presented with four of the music industry's best-known awards, Grammys. *Private Dancer* won Best Album, "What's Love Got to Do With It?" won Song of the Year, and Tina Turner was awarded Top Vocalist in both the rock and the pop categories.

This was her crowning crossover. No one was wondering where Ike was, no one was looking at her skin, they were hearing her voice. The girl singing rhythm and blues the way Ike Turner had wanted was now producing her own special sounds. "I don't want to beg and plead anymore," she declared. "I had enough of that."

Music critic Cathleen McGuigan noticed that "Where her frenzied performances were once to release private frustrations, she says she now sings from strength and pleasure in her independence. . . . Her songs are fueled by the emotional resonance of a grown woman, not the attention-grabbing antics of a teenager."

After a lifetime of working and waiting, at long last Tina was at the wheel, directing her own career to success after success. Tina's song as Aunty Entity, "We Don't Need Another Hero," hit No. 2 in the U.S. charts. Tina's naturally forceful personality lends itself to her role alongside Mel Gibson in the Mad Max *movie.*

Hollywood offers

In June 1985, Tina's movie, *Mad Max: Beyond Thunderdome* was released. Her performance as Aunty Entity thrilled the audiences. The music video to the film, "We Don't Need Another Hero," sung by Tina, filled the airwaves. In July, Tina shared the stage with her old friend Mick Jagger, and the pair of them brought the house down for the all-star Live Aid benefit concert. Nineteen eighty-five closed with Tina's achievements being applauded by the presentation of another award. This was from the National Association for the Advancement of

Colored People (N.A.A.C.P.), acknowledging Tina as Best Actress for her performance in *Mad Max*.

Offers for other Hollywood roles rolled in, but Tina knew enough to be choosy. When Steven Spielberg asked her three times to take the lead role in his movie, *The Color Purple*, Tina declined, saying that she had lived that story too much to want to portray it. "I'm waiting for good scripts," she announced. "It's tougher for a black woman to get good parts. But at least now everyone in California knows I want to act, so it's just a matter of waiting." Not only did Tina want to act; she could.

Meanwhile, Ike moved back to his home town of Clarksdale, Mississippi. Yet the fast Hollywood lifestyle had its hooks into him, and he couldn't shake himself free from drugs. He was arrested for possession of cocaine and given a one year jail sentence in the state of California.

Tina's tale

In 1986, Tina was offered $400,000 for her success story and, in July the book, *I, Tina*, appeared on the stands and became a bestseller. Just as her second solo album, *Break Every Rule*, sold over 300,000 copies and turned platinum, Touchstone Pictures bought the film rights to *I, Tina*. It seemed as though Tina Turner was unstoppable.

Far from the limelight, Tina found romance with a German record executive named Erwin Bach. Erwin was as young as Tina's sons, but age posed no barrier to love. At last Tina felt happy. In their years together, living in Europe, Tina and Erwin had no plans to marry. Tina divided her time and attention between Hollywood and their various homes across Europe – at different times they lived in England, France, Monaco, and Cologne in Germany.

In her busy schedule, Tina found time to visit places of cultural interest, as well as to chant daily. Sensible, moderate eating kept her in good health. "I used to eat a lot of pork, fried foods and bread. I just love bread with lots of butter. But, I've learned moderation. I really do think that's it for anything. It won't matter how long you work out at the gym if

Below: The Caribbean island of Grenada acknowledges Tina Turner and her achievements by dedicating a stamp to her.

Bottom: Tina's escort is Ervin Bach. Tina made her home with Ervin in Europe claiming, "We're as married as we need to be. It's a great, comfortable relationship."

55

This page and opposite: Records of success; a string of Tina Turner's albums tracks her growth as she re-established her career as a performing artist. Tina's third solo album, Foreign Affair, *is the first to feature Tina as a producer and musical arranger. Released in September 1989, it entered the British charts . . . at No. 1.* Simply the Best *appeared in September 1991, much to the delight of Tina's dedicated fans, selling over four million copies.*

you're doing the same unhealthy things when you come out of there," she advised.

In March 1987, Tina embarked on the *Break Every Rule* world tour. In August she was singing in America, in January she was in Argentina, in March she finished in Osaka, Japan. Four million fans heard Tina in concert. In thirteen of the twenty-five countries visited, Tina broke box office records. In Europe, her ticket sales were higher than those of another superstar, Madonna.

In 1989, Tina released another album, *Foreign Affair*. This album was the first to feature Tina as both arranger and producer. She was taking a more creative role and was more in charge of her music. Always expanding her expertise, Tina also performed at an AIDS benefit in London with the British comedian John Cleese. After this performance, Tina added comedy to her array of talents.

From strength to strength

Foreign Affair outsold *Private Dancer* in Britain and went platinum several times over as it sold out in fourteen countries across the globe. In 1990, the *Foreign Affair* tour started in Belgium, and when it finished in Rotterdam, Tina had played to more fans across Europe than any other superstar. The 3.5 million fans were delighted and Tina Turner showed no signs of slowing down.

Next page: Supported by
a superb rock band,
swathed in the latest
fashions, and bathed in
dancing spotlights, Tina
conquers the stage at
the Maracana Stadium,
Brazil. Singing her way
into her fifth decade,
Tina Turner showed
that she was still the
queen of rock.

In September 1991, Tina, aged fifty-
one, released *Simply the Best*, an album
of her greatest hits. It hit No.1 in Britain and sold
over four million copies worldwide. In 1992, Tina
started recording with Virgin Records in the United
States. Her debut album under the new label was
What's Love Got to Do With It? The release, in 1993,
coincided with the release of Touchstone's movie by
the same name starring Angela Bassett, as Tina, and
Larry Fishburne, as Ike.

I, Tina

It was quite difficult to impersonate the legend of
Tina Turner. "She's this beautiful, gorgeous woman
with incredible energy," Bassett said. "When I met
her at the studio, she looked at me and said, 'She's
gorgeous.' We embraced and she started showing me
pictures of her and the Ikettes. When I left, I was
energized. I was inspired to do my best. I wanted to
convey that she is a bright woman, a survivor and a
fighter." One film critic revealed, "Hollywood hasn't
produced many films about strong women lately; this
one is a happy exception. It'll certainly make you
want to root for this lady who flat-out refuses to sing
the blues. . . . Tina's an angel with wigs – and a beat
that just won't quit."

"It was hard for me," said Tina, "but I think it is
possible for us as people to deal with more than we

*"... the real power
behind whatever
success I have now was
something I found
within myself –
something that's in all
of us, I think, a piece of
God just waiting to be
discovered."*

Tina Turner.

know. I believe we have the power to endure a lot. I've gone through a lot in my life, but I've managed to turn it around."

At fifty-five, Tina Turner showed no signs of stopping, or even slowing down. Her years of performing had kept her toned and slim. Tina Turner stood as singing and dancing proof that age need not be a huge obstacle to active living. As the "grandmother" of rock, Tina gave powerful lessons about music, determination, and dignity to younger generations; she became a citizen of the world, delighting audiences across the globe. Against the odds of an unhappy childhood and a desperate marriage, Tina Turner reigned supreme.

Glossary

Arranger: Someone who adapts existing music for different instruments or writes accompanying passages of music for a record.

Bass line: The lowest part in a musical piece that is made up of different rhythmic parts.

Blues: An African-American style of music that originates from rural southern America. It is often improvised and is based on repetitive musical patterns. It relies on a moody, vocal performance with the name "the blues" describing the feeling of the song or music. The style was very influential in the development of pop, *jazz*, rock, and classical music.

Boogie-woogie: A blues style of playing, usually on the piano, relying on a heavy rhythmic *bass line* being played with the left hand. Popular in the 1940s, it influenced the development of *rock and roll*.

Buddhism: A religion that originated in India based on the teachings of Buddha. Its main belief is of karma – that there is just reward or punishment for the way a person has behaved either in this life or in the life to come.

Charts: The music industry's weekly listing and ranking of the most played songs, divided by category, e.g. pop, *soul* and *rock and roll*.

Cherokee: A Native American tribe of people originally living in what is now Tennessee and North Carolina.

Cover: A new version of an already existing record by a different singer or group.

Domestic violence: Violence that occurs among family members or within the confines of a private home.

Gig: A live performance or musical engagement for a musician or band.

Gold disc: A symbolic gold record, presented to a musician when 400,000 copies of a single, or 100,000 copies of an album, have been sold.

Gospel: Vocal music that originated with African American church-goers in the southern states of America in the 1920s. This type of music was a cross-fertilization of the hymn, *blues*, and *jazz*.

Grammy: An annual musical award in the United States, presented in recognition of achievement in forty different musical categories.

Integration: The process whereby a minority group mixes with, and is accorded equal rights to, the majority society.

Jazz: A style of music developed in the southern states of America in the early twentieth century. It is characterized by its improvised style and *syncopated* rhythm, and is a blending of worldwide cultural influences found in work songs, *spirituals, ragtime,* and *blues*.

"Jim Crow": Any law or policy relating to *segregation* and discrimination against black people in the U.S.

Navajo: A Native American people who originally lived in what is now Arizona, in the United States.

On the road: A term used in the music industry when musicians and bands are touring to give concerts.

Platinum disc: A symbolic platinum record presented to a musician or singer when 600,000 copies of a single, or 300,000 copies of an album, have been sold.

Producer: The person who oversees the sound and feel of a record in production.

Ragtime: A musical style characterized by *syncopation* and simple melodies. These were originally for piano, and were made popular by Scott Joplin in the 1890s.

Rhythm and blues (R&B): Popular African American music that originated in the south of the United States between the 1940s and 1960s. The style is a combination of *blues* and *jazz* and was a predecessor to *soul* music.

Rock and roll: A style of music influenced by *rhythm and blues* and country and western music. It has a strong beat and is usually played on amplified instruments.

Royalty: An agreed percentage of the price of a record that is paid to the artist by the publisher or record company every time a copy of the record is sold.

Segregation: The establishment by law or custom of separate facilities for ethnic or social groups, such as the *Jim Crow* laws.

Soul: A style of music that is full of emotion, dating from the 1960s. Its influences are *rhythm and blues* and *gospel*.

Spirituals: A type of religious song that occurred when the African slaves became exposed to Christianity in America. The songs were influenced by hymns, but freer in melody and rhythm.

Syncopation: When stress is placed on the usually weaker beat, as opposed to the stronger one, in a musical piece.

Synthesizer: An electronic device that can produce a wide variety of sounds. It became widely used in the rock music industry, replacing many traditional instruments.

Index

INTERNATIONAL SCHOOL OF LONDON

139 Gunnersbury Ave.
London
W3 8LG